A NOTE OF THANKS

A NOTE OF THANKS

the art of gratitude

DOMINIQUE DEVITO

STERLING
INNOVATION
A Division of Sterling Publishing, Inc.
New York

Library of Congress Cataloging-in-Publication Data

DeVito, Dominique C.
  A note of thanks : the art of gratitude / Dominique DeVito.
      p. cm.
  Includes bibliographical references.
  ISBN-13: 978-1-4027-4691-8
  ISBN-10: 1-4027-4691-1
  1.Thank-you notes. 2.Letter writing.   I.Title.

BJ2115.T45D48 2007
395.4--dc22

                        2006038956

10 9 8 7 6 5 4 3 2 1

Published by Sterling Publishing Co., Inc.
387 Park Avenue South, New York, NY 10016
© 2007 by Sterling Publishing Co., Inc.
Distributed in Canada by Sterling Publishing
c/o Canadian Manda Group, 165 Dufferin Street
Toronto, Ontario, Canada M6K 3H6
Distributed in the United Kingdom by GMC Distribution Services
Castle Place, 166 High Street, Lewes, East Sussex, England BN7 1XU
Distributed in Australia by Capricorn Link (Australia) Pty. Ltd.
P.O. Box 704, Windsor, NSW 2756, Australia

Manufactured in the United States of America

Design by Gabriela Gasparini

Sterling ISBN-13: 978-1-4027-4691-8
        ISBN-10: 1-4027-4691-1

For information about custom editions, special sales, premium and
corporate purchases, please contact Sterling Special Sales
Department at 800-805-5489 or specialsales@sterlingpub.com.

CONTENTS

CHAPTER ONE
An Historical Perspective on Etiquette and Letter Writing

"Gratitude is our most direct line to God and the angels. If we take the time, no matter how crazy and troubled we feel, we can find something to be thankful for. The more we seek gratitude, the more reason the angels will give us for gratitude and joy to exist in our lives."
—*Terry Lynn Taylor*

It's fascinating to think that for generations, people have taken pen to paper to craft notes of thanks—and other kinds of letters—just as you do (or want to do!) today. In fact, it is no accident that writing thank-you notes is as important in our time as it was for our ancestors. Even with the faster and more varied ways we have of communicating, nothing beats the personalized thank-you note, when it's called for. The reasons for this are steeped in the traditions of etiquette. Let's take a look.

Etiquette is a French word meaning "ticket." Etiquettes were first used by Louis XIV's gardener in the king's palace at Versailles, outside of Paris, where he posted tickets to tell people to "Stay Off the Grass." When no one paid much attention, the frustrated gardener went to the king himself and complained long and loud enough that His Majesty issued an edict for everyone in the court to keep within the "etiquettes." Eventually the term came to cover proper demeanor in court circles in France and then around the world. Even after empires and monarchies fell, people still looked to the aristocratic class to help define social practices.

In her 1922 book on etiquette—*Etiquette in Society, in Business, in Politics, and at Home*—the now-famous Emily Post included an introduction by Richard Duffy that observed:

> People who ridicule etiquette as a mass of trivial and arbitrary conventions, extremely troublesome to those who practise them and insupportable to everybody else, seem to forget the long,

slow progress of social intercourse in the upward climb of man from the primeval state.

Conventions were established from the first to regulate the rights of the individual and the tribe. They were and are the rules of the game of life and must be followed if we would "play the game." Ages before man felt the need of indigestion remedies, he ate his food solitary and furtive in some corner, hoping he would not be espied by any stronger and hungrier fellow. It was a long, long time before the habit of eating in common was acquired; and it is obvious that the practise could not have been taken up with safety until the individuals of the race knew enough about one another and about the food resources to be sure that there was food sufficient for all. When eating in common became the vogue, table manners made their appearance and they have been waging an uphill struggle ever since.

Duffy's language is strong, revealing a deep commitment to the importance of manners. Most books of this kind were and still are written this way so that the reader, as well, takes the message seriously. Duffy goes on to say:

> The custom of raising the hat when meeting an acquaintance derives from the old rule that friendly knights in accosting each other should raise the visor for mutual recognition in amity. In the knightly years, it must be remembered, it was important to know whether one was meeting friend or foe. Meeting a foe meant fighting on the spot. Thus, it is evident that the conventions of courtesy not only tend to make the wheels of life run more smoothly, but also act as safeguards in human relationship.

The "convention of courtesy" to which this book is devoted is the art of writing thank-you notes. This practice became firmly established in the Victorian era of calling cards, when, according to Emily Post, "...with a hair-pin and a visiting card, [a woman] is ready to meet most emergencies." She notes in her 1922 book:

> Although the principal use of a visiting card, at least the one for which it was originally invented—to be left as an evidence of one person's presence at the house of another—is going gradually out of ardent favor in fashionable circles, its usefulness seems to keep a nicely adjusted balance. In New York, for instance, the visiting card has entirely taken the place of the written note of invitation to informal parties of every description.

THE EVOLUTION AND DEVOLUTION OF CALLING CARDS

Visiting cards, also known as calling cards, first appeared in China in the fifteenth century and became popular in France before spreading throughout Europe in the seventeenth century.

Calling cards were engraved with the caller's name and address, and were left by people wanting to expand their social circles at the homes of those of social, artistic, or political prominence.

Ladies "called" in their carriages and most often left their cards with someone's butler or other household servant. Likewise, while a lady was out, her butler or servant accepted cards from callers. Soon, a whole set of customs grew around the practice. For example:

✳ When the lady of the house received a card from a caller, she would decide whether to receive him or her. Etiquette dictated that the caller not inquire whether anyone was at home, but rather await word as to whether he or she would be seen.

✳ If the caller was told that the lady of the house was not home, it was considered a rejection. If a reciprocal card from the lady of the house was not given to the caller (as a gesture of politeness to indicate that a visit at a later time might be possible), he or she could assume that there was no interest on the part of the mistress in developing the relationship.

✳ By the mid 1800s, when a wife would make a call, she would leave her own card plus two of her husband's—one each for the mistress and the master of the house she was calling upon. Daughters who were of age and who joined their mothers on calls would have their names engraved on the cards, as well, and sometimes the names of all the children were featured.

✳ Calls were only to be made on days when it was known the mistress of the house was home—information that was usually engraved on the calling cards. New residents who were called upon and given others' cards then knew that it was appropriate to visit their new neighbors.

Engagements, births, deaths, and marriages typically required formal visits—typically within a week of the event. Polite callers knew not to overextend their welcome, usually visiting for thirty minutes or less. If another caller stopped in while one was there, the first was expected to leave shortly.

In Victorian times, the presentation and design of a card indicated a great deal to the receiver. A folded top-left corner meant the visitor had come in person, a folded top-right corner meant congratulations, and a folded lower-right corner expressed sympathy. An unfolded card meant a servant was sent. A black band around the edge signified that the carrier was in mourning. If a card featured the initials P.P.C. (*Pour Prendre Congé*), the recipient knew that the caller was planning to "take leave" of the area for a period of time.

Servants and footmen became instrumental in the flutter of card giving and receiving, confining the practice to those who could afford to employ such aides. It was the servants who accepted the cards and the footmen who delivered them, but the lady of the house was responsible for providing a response and arranging visits.

In the United States, the use of calling cards blossomed after the Civil War, even though they had previously been considered old European affectations. When the practice came back in style, American ladies embraced it, which led to the establishment of certain rules of etiquette regarding the distribution of cards, how the cards were supposed to look, and what kinds of trays were to be used to receive them.

The practice of leaving and receiving calling cards eventually waned along with the disappearance of the servant class. Although a different code of social etiquette is followed today, one social grace that has not completely fallen by the wayside—and that is still considered essential—is the writing of thank-you notes and other cards of congratulations, sympathy, and announcement.

"Our favorite attitude should be gratitude."
—*Anonymous*

THOUGHTS ON LETTER WRITING
IN THE EARLY 1900S

Joseph Devlin contributed to the etiquette of letter writing in this country with his 1910 book *How to Speak and Write Correctly.* He observed:

> Many people seem to regard letter-writing as a very simple and easily acquired branch, but on the contrary it is one of the most difficult forms of composition and requires much patience and labor to master its details. In fact there are very few perfect letter-writers in the language. It constitutes the direct form of speech and may be called conversation at a distance. Its forms are so varied by every conceivable topic written at all times by all kinds of persons in all kinds of moods and tempers and addressed to all kinds of persons of varying degrees in society and of different pursuits in life, that no fixed rules can be laid down to regulate its length, style or subject matter. Only general suggestions can be made in regard to scope and purpose, and the forms of indicting

set forth which custom and precedent have sanctioned.

The principles of letter-writing should be understood by everybody who has any knowledge of written language, for almost everybody at some time or other has necessity to address some friend or acquaintance at a distance, whereas comparatively few are called upon to direct their efforts towards any other kind of composition.

Formerly the illiterate countryman, when he had occasion to communicate with friends or relations, called in the peripatetic schoolmaster as his amanuensis, but this had one drawback—secrets had to be poured into an ear other than that for which they were intended, and often the confidence was betrayed.

Now, that education is abroad in the land, there is seldom any occasion for any person to call upon the service of another to compose and write a personal letter. Very few now-a-days are so grossly illiterate as not to be able to read and write. No matter how crude his effort may be it is better for any one to write his own letters than trust to another. Even if he should commence— "deer fren, i lift up my pen to let ye no that I hove been sik for the past 3 weeks, hopping this will find ye the same," his spelling and construction can be excused in view of the fact that his intention is good, and that he is doing his best to serve his own turn without depending upon others.

The nature, substance and tone of any letter depend upon the occasion that calls it forth, upon the person writing it and upon the person for whom it is intended. Whether it should be easy or formal in style, plain or ornate, light or serious, gay or grave, sentimental or matter-of-fact depend upon these three circumstances.

Devlin's timeless thoughts on what constitute an appropriate letter are reflected throughout this book and are themes you'll be reminded of as you read the sections on the following pages that pertain to the kind of note you want to write. These include using a tone and style that's consistent with both the occasion for the note writing, and with how well you know the person to whom you're sending the card. Devlin continues:

> In letter writing the first and most important requisites are to be natural and simple; there should be no straining after effect, but simply a spontaneous out-pouring of thoughts and ideas as they naturally occur to the writer. We are repelled by a person who is stiff and labored in his conversation and in the same way the stiff and labored letter bores the reader. Whereas if it is light and in a conversational vein it immediately engages his attention.

The letter which is written with the greatest facility is the best kind of letter because it naturally expresses what is in the writer, he has not to search for his words, they flow in a perfect unison with the ideas he desires to communicate. When you write to your friend John Browne to tell him how you spent Sunday you have not to look around for the words, or study set phrases with a view to please or impress Browne, you just tell him the same as if he were present before you, how you spent the day, where you were, with whom you associated and the chief incidents that occurred during the time. Thus, you write natural and it is such writing that is adapted to epistolary correspondence.

There are different kinds of letters, each calling for a different style of address and composition, nevertheless the natural key should be maintained in all, that is to say, the writer should never attempt to convey an impression that he is other than what he is. Still the writer should keep in mind the person to whom he is writing. If it is to an Archbishop or some other great dignitary of Church or state it certainly should be couched in terms different from those he uses to John Browne, his intimate friend. Just as he cannot say "Dear John" to an Archbishop, no more can he address him in the familiar words he uses to his friend of everyday acquaintance and companionship. Yet there is no great learning required to write to an Archbishop, no more than to an ordinary individual. All the laborer needs to know is the form of address and how to properly utilize his limited vocabulary to the best advantage.

Despite the tactile and reflective pleasure of taking pen to paper to write a note or letter, there is no denying that e-mailing is the preferred method of communication for most people these days. Just as the purveyors of manners at the turn of the last century made sure that we were minding our P's and Q's when it came to sending letters, so today there are numerous individuals and groups that provide guidelines for communicating properly via electronic mail. There's even a term for it: netiquette (network etiquette).

Netiquette addresses the issues of making the most of the subject line of your e-mail, who should or shouldn't be cc'd or bcc'd, rules for personal and business correspondence, use of symbols such as smiley faces (called emotions), and use of abbreviated text, most commonly used in text messages.

The purpose of this book, however, is to help you master the art of "old-fashioned" letter writing, using what sometimes may feel like antiquated tools: pen and paper. Although, as mentioned, we have choices in how we communicate, I hope you'll discover—through writing thank-you notes—the simple pleasure of taking time with your thoughts, carefully addressing an envelope and selecting a stamp, and fully experiencing the act of expressing gratitude, which sustains us and our relationships.

CHAPTER TWO
Why We Should Write Thank-You Notes

"A good deed is never lost. He who sows courtesy, reaps friendship; he who plants kindness, gathers love; pleasure bestowed on a grateful mind was never sterile, but generally gratitude begets reward." —*St. Basil*

Is there anything more wonderful than collecting the day's mail and finding among the bills, magazines, and junk mail that rarity of things, the handwritten letter? All the day's worries are cast aside as the envelope is opened and the personal message is revealed. Receiving a letter is like getting a surprise package whose contents are personalized for you alone. What a gift!

Once upon a time, before text messages, e-mails, telephones, beepers, faxes, and all the other ways of communicating instantly with others, there was one tried-and-true way to get your message to someone: the mail. Imagine knowing that you had to wait days, weeks, and sometimes longer to get even a simple message through the mail to someone. Your need to communicate grew only more intense as you anticipated both the reaction of the receiver and the eagerly awaited reply.

Our modern ways of communicating instantly are a great boon to personal, social, and business relationships, and there's certainly no going back. But why isn't it enough to just say thank you, or to call and thank someone, or to send an e-card? First, because certain occasions require thank-you notes, a practice that dates back to the days of frequent social visits. Any of the numerous books on etiquette you may find at a library or bookstore will include instructions for when it is appropriate to write a thank-you note (not to worry, this book covers all the bases). Second, because sending a handwritten thank-you note is the sincerest form of expressing gratitude, and when someone does something nice for you, your note is the simple act of kindness returned.

BETTER THAN A PHONE CALL

Some things we have grown to take for granted, like the receipt of a care package at college or camp, or even a birthday present that arrives from an old friend. These gifts are usually acknowledged in a phone call. While a call is nice, it is even nicer for the person who sent you the gift to receive a letter like the following:

Dear Emma,

I was so happy to come home from work and find something in the mail other than bills and junk mail. It was an envelope from you, decorated with one of your signature flowers—a treat in itself. When I opened it and found the gift certificate to my favorite bookstore, I was absolutely tickled. The new Sue Grafton mystery is out, and I have been wanting to read it. I am going to the store tonight to pick it up.

You made my day. Thank you so much!
All my love,
Alison

Dear Mom,

It was so cool to get your package at the dorm today. It made my day. When I opened it up to find a box of your awesome oatmeal cookies plus a special coffee mug and a bag of my favorite coffee, I felt like I was home again. I miss you, and the dogs. Thanks, Mom, and I'll see you in a few weeks.

Love,
Jack

A VALIANT— AND VALUABLE— GESTURE

A simple thank-you note can change the course of your life. The people who receive your notes of thanks are likely to think more highly of you and therefore assist you in ways you may not even realize. Some may be obvious, like continuing to receive special presents from grandparents, or being invited back to influential parties. Some may be less obvious, like having a personal reference written for you to a college you're eager to get into because you sent a thank-you note to your father's friend when he helped coach you in soccer. Here are some other examples where a thank-you note determined how the sender was treated:

✻ Paul didn't realize it, but he was one of three top candidates being considered for a plum entry-level job with a highly respected financial firm. Paul had good grades, strong recommendations, and a very successful interview process that had propelled him to the top of the pack. Not knowing whether he was a contender, Paul did know that the final step was to write a thank-you note. He was the only one of the three finalists who did, and for the company, that was enough to secure him the position.

✳ Sarah had just organized a major fundraiser for the school where she worked, securing donations from local businesses and individuals. She had thanked everyone over the phone who said they would send something, but she went the extra mile to send personal notes of thanks when the fundraiser was over. As a result, she received confirmations that she could count on many of the same businesses and people for similar contributions when she'd need them again.

✳ Connie called several insurance agencies to ask questions about what kind of policy might best suit her. There were things she liked and disliked about all of them. The agency that got her business was the one whose agent explained things thoroughly on the phone and followed up with a personal note thanking her for her interest and offering some additional information based on the conversation they'd had. According to Connie, "When I got that kind of attention from a simple query, I knew I'd be taken care of." She has happily been with the same company ever since.

✳ Sandra was eager to get to know her neighbors better when she moved into what seemed like a close-knit community. When she and her family were invited to a summer barbeque, she quickly called to say that they would come and asked the hostess if there was anything she could bring. The day of the picnic, she and her family arrived with a large salad. Everyone at the party was friendly and seemed equally pleased to meet Sandra and her family. When they left several hours later, they all felt much better about their new home and neighborhood. The next day, Sandra wrote a short but sincere thank-you note and dropped it at her neighbor's house. A few hours later the phone rang. It was her neighbor, thanking her for the note and inviting her for coffee later that week. They are now close friends.

JUST DO IT

Understanding all this may not help you overcome the anxiety you feel in actually writing a thank-you note. For most of us, possibly looking silly on paper, or not being able to find the right words, can keep us from ever writing to anyone. After all, expressing gratitude, kindness, and courtesy may seem awkward for some of us, even though it sounds good.

Like anything new that you want to learn, the only way to get started is with the desire to simply do it. Don't let procrastination get the better of you here. If you do, it'll make your job more difficult because you'll feel guilty, put more pressure on yourself, and risk sending a note so late that it'll be considered more rude than appropriate.

Writing a thank-you note is a simple act. Start small and feel good about each step you take, and your confidence will grow. Remember that thank-you notes are meant to be short, so you don't need to spend a lot of time writing them. Let your positive feelings for the gift you received, or for the simple act of kindness that's been done for you or a loved one, infuse the note with the sentiment you wish to express. The examples in the following chapters on specific kinds of notes to write in certain situations can serve as springboards to your own personal notes.

If you find that you have reservations about writing a letter that might keep you from following through with it, consider what may happen if you don't. You may lose a job or a client. You may turn off a neighbor (and there's nothing to make life more unbearable than a neighbor with whom you don't get along), upset a relative (causing family strife), hurt the feelings of an old friend, or be taken off an invitation list. You simply can't assume that an act of kindness can go unacknowledged, and you can't expect that the occasions that necessitate thank-you notes can be overlooked, no matter how busy, tired, stressed, or otherwise overwhelmed you may be.

You'll discover in this book that an appropriate thank-you note need not be the "letter of a lifetime" that will define who you are for someone forever (although it perhaps could be). The great thing about thank-you notes is that as long as you are expressing yourself sincerely, the person you give or send the note to will be so touched that he or she will forgive what you might feel are big mistakes—misspelled words, awkward sentences, and so on. Just completing a note—saying what you want to say, securing it in an envelope, and sending or giving it to its intended party—is enough. This book is full of examples of notes that may not be perfect on paper, but were perfect for those who received them.

"Develop an attitude of gratitude, and give thanks for everything that happens to you, knowing that every step forward is a step toward achieving something bigger and better than your current situation." —*Brian Tracy*

Words and Phrases to Get You Started

If you feel there's no way you can sound as eloquent as even one of the basic examples in this book, the first thing you need to do is think again, because you definitely can. The second thing is to go ahead and use the examples in this book to get started. Here are some simple ways to get a thank-you note started that always sound good.

✳ I just want to say thank you.

✳ I just want to say thanks.

✳ Thank you so much for the...

✳ My sincerest thanks for the...

✳ I can't thank you enough for...

✳ Thank you, from the
   bottom of my heart.

✳ Thank you for seeing me today.

✳ Thank you for being there for me.

✳ Thank you for helping me with…

✳ Thank you for all you've done for…

✳ Thank you for your time.

As you'll learn later on, you want to be
as specific as possible about what it is
you're thanking someone for. The
phrases above are introductory and
should be followed by a description of
what your appreciation is for, specifically.

CHAPTER THREE
What You'll Need to Write Thank-You Notes

"When it comes to life, the critical thing is whether you take things for granted or take them with gratitude." —*G. K. Chesterton*

With inspiration as your guide, all you need to complete your thank-you notes are a few basic supplies: pen, paper, envelope, address, and stamp. That's it! And what's wonderful about the simplicity of your supply list is that there are so many variations of each—except the address, of course.

It's good to know a bit about the history of writing and how it evolved. A type of alphabet was developed some time between 1700 and 1500 B.C., but wasn't used extensively until about 600 B.C. The Greeks were the first to develop a writing system that went from left to right, in 400 B.C., and it was the Greeks, too, who fashioned a writing stylus—made of metal, bone, or ivory—to make marks on wax-coated tablets. It wasn't until nearly A.D. 1600—some two thousand years later—that writing instruments and materials became suitable enough to make writing practical, and the old Greek and Roman letterforms transformed into the twenty-six-letter alphabet we use today. Aldus Manutius, an Italian from Venice, is credited with inventing the "running hand" form of upper- and lowercase letters.

THE PEN

For some people, the only occasion to use a pen anymore is to jot down a note or make a list—and some even do these tasks electronically. Considering this, it is hard to even imagine that for over one thousand years the writing instrument of choice was the quill pen! The strongest quills were plucked from a specific part of a living bird's wing. Swan quills were the most luxurious, crow feathers provided the finest lines, and other feathers came from geese, eagles, owls, hawks, and even turkeys. The quills were successful because they were hollow and could absorb and contain a small amount of ink. They could also be cut to form a tip, producing a thin or thick line of ink. Our ancestors needed to sharpen their quills with a knife (thus the term "pen knife") and use a coal stove to dry the ink they used on whatever crude form of writing material was available. Quills lasted about a week, depending on how frequently they were used.

The oldest version of a fountain pen, which mimicked the quill's natural ink reserve, dates back to 1702, and was created by a Frenchman named M. Bion. In the 1800s, development of a more reliable writing instrument really took off. In 1809, Peregrine Williamson, an American from Baltimore, received a patent for a steel pen; in 1831, John Jacob Parker patented the first self-filling fountain pen; and in 1884, the first practical fountain pen, created by Lewis Waterman, a New York City salesman, was patented. The story goes that Waterman was inspired to come up with a better writing instrument after a leaky pen destroyed one of his valuable sales contracts.

Self-filling soft rubber cartridges made the popular pen styles of the early 1900s more practical. In 1938, the ballpoint pen, which used a small ball bearing in its tip to control the flow of ink from a cartridge, was invented by a Hungarian journalist named Laszlo Biro. It used quicker-drying newspaper ink, making it even more practical. During World War II, the British Royal Air Force was looking for a pen that wouldn't leak at high altitudes, and bought the licensing rights for the patent from Biro.

Between the early 1940s and late 1950s, a battle of sorts played out between pen manufacturers to capture the popular market for ballpoints. During this time, Eberhard-Faber developed its Eversharp CA; Reynolds launched its Reynolds Rocket (which had sales of more than $100,000 on its first day; the BIC pen was introduced by the French; and Parker created the Jotter, the first retractable ballpoint pen. By 1960, BIC was dominating the European market, and, after buying Waterman Pens in the United States, was able to introduce ballpoints that sold for between 30 and 70 cents a piece. Today, there are more than ten million BICs sold daily worldwide.

You can enjoy the ballpoint revolution and use a tried-and-true blue or black pen as your writing instrument of choice, or you can have fun exploring other options. There are all kinds of ballpoint pens, fountain pens, "roller" pens, and markers that can help you get your message across. A visit to an office supply store or stationery store can at least familiarize you with the popular choices; exploring the world of designer pens online or in select retailers is something you may even find yourself getting into. Just as when you were a child, it was fun to go from trying the pack of sixty-four crayons to the box that had more than one hundred different colors, so as an adult it can be fun to go from using a couple of pens that you may like to having a whole collection.

You may find that different inks work better on different papers, or that you like the look of a metallic pen for certain occasions, or that the feel of a wood-handled pen is nicer than plastic or metal. Your tastes may change, too, as time goes by, and the world of personalized stationery and stationery products will be there to accommodate you, as it's always evolving, as well.

Ink-credible

The Chinese made the greatest strides in developing ink as a writing medium. The first known ink—commonly used back in 1200 B.C.—was a combination of pine-smoke soot, lamp oil, and gelatin from donkey skin and musk. Inks were also developed from berries, plants, and minerals. A formula that was a mix of iron salts, nutgalls, and gum was developed around A.D. 400 and was used for centuries. Today, inks come in a slew of colors for both artistic and recreational uses. It's fun to experiment with different colors, but remember that unless you know the person very well, it's best to use traditional colors when writing thank-you notes.

THE PAPER

Stone or baked-earth tablets, bark, wax, and animal skins were used by our ancient ancestors to write on. Papyrus—the skin of the papyrus reed that grows abundantly along the Nile Delta—was introduced by the Egyptians, and the oldest papyrus document discovered dates to 2000 B.C. In A.D. 105, a Chinese court official invented making paper from the byproducts of textile production, which led to the way paper has been made ever since. Basically, you need a durable material like wood that can be smashed into tiny pieces and made into a kind of soup. The liquid is poured onto a breathable mesh surface (typically a wire mesh) that allows it to be pressed and dried, forming large or small sheets of paper. Different kinds of wood make different kinds of paper. Other plants can even contribute to the papermaking process so that different results are obtained. There is paper made from cotton and linen, and paper made from synthetic materials.

While it took centuries to refine papermaking to produce a clean, flat sheet, papermakers have always reveled in the individuality of certain elements that allows them to produce distinctive types of paper. Some of these are obvious—a paper bag has a different look, feel, and function than a piece of copy paper, for example—and some of them aren't. The paper that books are printed on varies considerably, depending on how much ink may be going on the paper (full-color, heavily illustrated books need thicker, stronger paper), what type of book it is (a text-book or a paperback, for example), and even the kind of reading experience the publisher wants you to have (thicker, softer paper translates into a richer experience).

PAPER, GLORIOUS PAPER

While the recipient of your note may not know whether you used a one-thousand-dollar Mont Blanc or a two-dollar gel roller to write your card, he or she will have a different experience with your paper or card selection. Like pens, though, papers and the cards they're made into come in an almost overwhelming selection, from the most formal of wedding invitations to the most purely functional of notebooks. For thank-you notes, in particular, there are many preprinted cards that say "Thank You" in fancy lettering on the front, or as a fun greeting inside, such as "Fangs a lot for the Halloween party." Because of this, it's important to consider the kind of paper or card you choose so that it's appropriate to the recipient. The following chart provides a frame of reference, and there is even huge variety within these guidelines.

Occasion	Classification	Paper Type	Card Type
Wedding, Shower, New Baby	Formal	Heavy Stock, monogrammed if desired	Classic to match invitation stock if possible; can be printed to say "Thank You" on the front or inside
Business	Formal	Heavy Stock, monogrammed if desired	Classic—if printed on front be elective in type style to reflect nature of company (wealthy, playful, grass roots, etc.)

Occasion	Classification	Paper Type	Card Type
General gift	Formal Informal	If formal, see Wedding or Business, above; if informal, should be special stationery, though the design can be of your choosing	If formal, see Wedding or Businness, above; if informal, can be almost any style so long as it makes a nice presentation
Hospitality	Informal	Your choice	Your choice
Condolence	Formal	Fine stationery	Plain card of select stationery, or card with appropriate greeting
General	Informal	Your choice	Your choice
Kindness	Informal	Your choice	Your choice
From a child	Informal	Child can choose	Child can choose

MONOGRAMMED STATIONERY

There is something simple and elegant about stationery that has your name or initials on it. If this hasn't been something you've owned in the past, consider ordering some for yourself. In fact, if you have a big event like a wedding coming up, a classic monogrammed card will make the job of writing thank-yous much simpler, as it is appropriate to send to a diverse group of people, from long-lost relatives and business associates to close friends.

To select and order monogrammed stationery, visit a stationery store or explore your options online.

Emily Post discusses the importance of paper in *Etiquette in Society, in Business, and at Home*. She advises:

> Suitability should be considered in choosing note paper, as well as in choosing a piece of furniture for a house. For a handwriting which is habitually large, a larger sized paper should be chosen than for writing which is small. The shape of

paper should also depend somewhat upon the spacing of the lines which is typical of the writer, and whether a wide or narrow margin is used. Low, spread-out writing looks better on a square sheet of paper; tall, pointed writing looks better on paper that is high and narrow. Selection of paper whether rough or smooth is entirely a matter of personal choice—so that the quality be good, and the shape and color conservative.

DECORATING YOUR NOTE

If you're sending a card to a special family member or a friend, or if the card is coming from a child, you may want to further personalize it by decorating the card or the envelope. While you can add any decoration—by coloring on the card or envelope, or using stamps or stickers—you should be careful that your artwork doesn't over-power your written message. This is not a concern if the note is from a young child, for whom the drawing will tell the story. In all other instances, your embellishment must be used only as a decorative touch. If you want to create a drawing or painting for someone, you may want to consider doing so on a separate piece of paper and including it with your card.

THE ENVELOPE

Typically a box of cards or stationery comes with envelopes. But like paper, envelopes can be bought individually to match or color-coordinate with a particular paper color or style, and they range from the highly stylized (sometimes lined with multiple sheets of thin colored paper on the inside) to the purely practical that are bought in economical boxes. Either choice beats wrapping your note in animal skin, or baking it in clay, like the Babylonians did centuries ago.

Although envelopes have become somewhat standardized (for the benefit of postal systems worldwide), they can still be personalized. As with the thank-you note, artwork is something that can be used to embellish your envelope if you're sending a special thank-you to a family member or friend. A more formal thank-you note can be sealed with a wax seal and stamp, a tradition that harkens back to notices sent by members of royalty. Because wax seals are likely to break off in the sorting machines used at post offices, stickers have been created to replicate them. While you may not have a family crest that you can use, you can find all sorts of fanciful designs and alphabet letters in different type faces.

What follows is Emily Post's meticulous take on the envelope:

> The flap of the envelope should be plain and the point not unduly long. If the flap is square instead of being pointed, it may be allowed greater length without being eccentric. Colored linings to envelopes are at present in fashion. Thin white paper, with monogram or address stamped in gray to match gray tissue lining of the envelope is, for instance, in very best taste. Young girls may be allowed quite gay envelope linings, but the device on the paper must be minute, in proportion to the gaiety of the color.

Addressing Envelopes

How an address is presented on the envelope can set the tone for the letter inside. Your handwriting is, of course, the most telling part of the package and will instantly identify you if the person to whom you are writing knows you well. If you are writing to a stranger, you should take care to write as neatly as possible.

Depending on who will receive your letter, you will need to present the address formally or informally. If you've written a fairly formal note, you should address the envelope formally, as well, by spelling out as much of the information as possible. If your note is to a special someone or a friend, you can be less formal and not use a title, and you can certainly use abbreviations.

Another consideration is where to put your return address. For thank-you notes, the best place to note your return address is on the envelope's back flap, which can be easily torn from the envelope and saved.

THE OFTEN-OVERLOOKED STAMP

Here's another way to make note-writing fun: picking the stamps! Just as your paper and pen can reflect your personality and that of the note's intended, so can the stamp. The United States Postal Service (USPS) regularly comes out with new stamps that portray a variety of subjects from cloudscapes, historical figures, comic book characters, works of art, crafts, and animals, to themes like breast cancer awareness and baseball sluggers. Who knows, you—and your kids—may develop an interest in stamp collecting that can last a lifetime and continue for generations.

These days, you can also create a personalized stamp with your favorite family photo. You can do this and see the range of styles offered by the post office either by asking a clerk at your local branch or going to the Web site of the USPS: www.usps.com.

The phrase "out of sight, out of mind" applies to writing paper, as well. Your best intentions will soon be replaced by the hassle of having to search for your paper and special pen if, when you go to write your thank-you note, you can't find them. If, however, you put your supplies in a special place, retrieving them at the necessary time will be fast and easy.

When you first make the commitment to be better about writing thank-you notes, or you're doing them for one large project like responding to gift givers, you may have only one style of note card. As your knack for sending thank-yous develops, you'll find that your collection of cards expands, too—conservative cards for people you may not know well or for more formal occasions, feminine cards for girlfriends, and fun cards for informal thank-yous. Your pen collection may grow, as well.

The best way to keep everything together in a special spot is to find a container for the collection. One container is best, even though you may be tempted to put pens or stickers in something else.

The kind of container you select can be as simple as a clear plastic bin or as fancy as an antique tin box. Be sure it's something that is reserved just for thank-you notes and, possibly, other letter-writing supplies. It might be a good idea to put a label on the box if it's going in a closet or drawer with other organizers like it.

READY, SET, WRITE!

You've visited stationery stores in your area and online, thoughtfully selected paper, envelopes, pens, stamps, and possibly some decorative touches, and put everything together where you can find it easily. There's nothing left now but to get started...with the help of the examples from this book! Relax; it may seem awkward at first, but once you get going, you'll feel great about your new endeavor to express gratitude, and you'll be dashing off meaningful thank-you notes in no time.

Before you get started, you should be aware that you may go through several pieces of paper or cards before you feel that your note says what you want it to. It may pain you to have to start over, but it is important that your note be as presentable as possible, especially if it's a follow-up to a job interview or other formal occasion. Using a piece of notebook or scrap paper to create your first drafts can save frustration and money.

CHAPTER FOUR
Thank-You Notes for Weddings and Related Events

"[There are] two kinds of gratitude: The sudden kind we feel for what we take; the larger kind we feel for what we give."
—*Edwin Arlington Robinson*

Being engaged is an exciting time to contemplate the kind of life you will build with your spouse. Why is it, then, that for all the times your heart races with joy at this occasion, there are nearly as many times when your heart races with…fear? There is so much to do to prepare for the wedding; so many questions to answer, so many decisions to be made. It is a busy, hectic time that is often punctuated by parties—bridal showers, bridesmaid parties, bachelor parties, family get-togethers, and office showers. You will be the recipient of gifts and well wishes, and you will need to do your part to let everyone know that you're grateful.

Every bride should keep careful lists and be well organized when it comes to sending thank-you notes. Brides typically receive gifts from early on in their engagement right through the first year of marriage, and these must all be acknowledged with thank-you notes. Take another look at the quote at the beginning of this chapter, and think about it when your enthusiasm is waning. You'll find that it will feel good to express your thanks in writing, and that those who receive your notes will be touched and delighted.

GIFTS GALORE

Take heart, brides! The custom of receiving gifts for your marriage is one that has existed for centuries. Way back when, brides needed to stock their new homes with everything that would allow them to live in the style to which they'd become accustomed—or at least with some token of what was important to her family. This was called a dowry. In more agrarian times, a dowry may have consisted of a piece of land or livestock. It may have included a couple of new dresses. Urban dowries were often loaded with the essentials for city living (and entertaining): china, silver, crystal, linens, and so on.

Dowries in Europe

The practice of providing a dowry—a contribution to the bride's household expenses—has been ongoing since the time of the Ancient Greeks. Also referred to as a "brideprice" in classical Greek times, it was common then for a smaller brideprice to be given by the groom to the bride's family. Similarly, in ancient Germany, a dowery was bestowed on the bride by the groom.

Failing to provide an acceptable or agreed-upon dowry could break off a marriage, and there were customs and rules for when brides could inherit parts of a dowry, particularly when it came to land.

For women who joined the church to become nuns, dowries were still provided by their families. A common form of charity was to offer dowries for poor women. The legend of St. Nicholas, which says that he threw gold into the stockings of three poor sisters as part of their dowries, led to the tradition of hanging and filling Christmas stockings.

For brides throughout the ages—just as for you—gifts will be given with the intention of helping you create a wonderful new home for you and your husband. Expect to be surprised by what that means to certain people, and remember, "Gratitude is the most exquisite form of courtesy," according to Jacques Maritain.

WHETHER, WHEN, AND HOW TO WRITE

If you're wondering whether a particular kind of wedding item necessitates a thank-you note, follow this simple rule: Whenever a gift is received for a wedding, shower, bachelor dinner, or any aspect of the engagement or wedding ceremony, it is customary to send a thank-you note.

If you're wondering how much time, after the event, you have to send your note, remember this: Codes of etiquette say that wedding gift thank-yous should be written within three months, though you'll certainly feel better and make the gift-givers happier if you send your cards within a few weeks.

So, with the inevitable before you, you may wonder about the best way to settle in and tackle the job. If possible, set up a station in your home or apartment that's reserved for this purpose. It may not seem like you'll need one, but your job will only be made more complicated if you need to dig around for your invite list, address book, note cards, and stamps every time you want to send a note. Keeping these supplies together and having a place set aside for them will save you valuable time and keep you focused on the task.

Hopefully, someone has made a detailed list of who gave what. Depending on how extensive your thank-you list is, you may want to break up the project so you don't get too tired and start short-changing your sentiments in the notes. One way to do this is to organize the list alphabetically by last name. Take one alphabet group per night and complete the task in a few days. Don't let a couple of days go by between groups, though, because you never know who may be comparing notes. Your aunt Katherine may ask your cousin Beth if she received a lovely thank-you note from the wedding. Even if she hasn't yet, if you've been working diligently, she will soon.

The secret to writing successful wedding thank-yous is to strike a balance between a form letter and a personal letter. The note has to follow some kind of standard form, otherwise it could take you months, not weeks, to say everything you may feel like saying to the special people who shared in your big day. On the other hand, if each note doesn't sound personal, the recipients will certainly notice, be assured, and your efforts, your time, and the cost of a stamp will be for naught. Here are some examples:

Dear Aunt Wendy,

Thank you so much for the lovely candlesticks. They are exquisite, and we plan to use them not just on special occasions, but every day so we can enjoy them. We hope you can come visit soon so we can share them with you, too.

It was so kind of you to come all the way to Memphis for the wedding. We were so happy to see you.

With all our love,
Sharon and Ken

A Note of Thanks

Dear Mr. and Dr. Laighty,

Thank you for your gift of the bread maker we registered for. We were so happy to receive it and look forward to many days of creating new and delicious bread recipes to share with our friends and family. This is something we really wanted, and we are grateful.

Sincerely,
Sharon and Ken Newbegin

You may come across some situations that you're not sure how to handle as you're writing your thank-you notes. These tips should help:

How to Address the Salutation

Use the gift-givers' first names, unless your relationship with them is formal or you don't know them well. For example, you may have always called your parents' friends down the street Mr. and Mrs. Adams. Even if you spent nearly every day at their house playing with their daughter, your best friend, now is not the time to address them as Ed and Sandy Adams. If you don't know the gift-givers well, you should address them by their last names. Formal salutations should also include someone's professional title (Dear Professor Larken or Dear Drs. John and Carrie Magrette). If the note is going to someone your spouse knows well but you don't, use the salutation that he would use.

How to Close the Note

The phrase you use to end your note should reflect your relationship with the gift-giver.

Some popular ones are Sincerely, Affectionately, Fondly, and With love. See page 122 for more suggestions.

How to Sign the Note

This seems like something obvious, but you'd be surprised how often people forget to do this! It's like making a birthday cake, frosting it, and forgetting the candles. There is a certain protocol to signing the note. For people you don't know well, sign your full name; for those you do know well, your first name alone suffices. If you've mentioned your spouse in the body of the note, you can sign for both of you (Linda and John Marywether).

Acknowledgments from Registries

Often when registries run out of an item, they send a note to indicate that it will be delayed. So that the gift-giver isn't left to come up with their own ideas about why they haven't heard from you, send a quick note to let them know what's happening and that you will be in touch again when the time comes. For example:

Dear Jill and Darren,

Just wanted to let you know that we received word from Pottery Barn that the glasses you ordered for us will be delivered in a couple of weeks. First, we are so pleased that you chose them for us. Second, we can't wait for you to enjoy them with us. We'll let you know when they arrive so that we can compare our calendars and schedule a date to get together.

Cheers!
Cindy and Russ

Some gifts are more difficult to personalize than others. After all, how effusive can you get over a place setting of your wedding china? In cases like these, think about how excited you were when you were choosing your wedding china and settings, and dream a little about what it will look like the first time you use it. Compare the following two notes:

Dear Rhonda,

Thank you so much for the set of sterling that goes with our wedding china. It was so nice of you to contribute to our future dinner parties. We hope to have one soon, and we'll be sending you an invitation.

Love,
Katie and Stan

Dear Rhonda,

What a delight to open your gift and find a set of sterling for our wedding china! Seeing it brought back so many happy memories of shopping for just the right set. Stan and I are excited about hosting many dinner parties with our special serving ware, and look forward to having you join us in making many more memories together. Thank you, too, for sharing our special day with us. It wouldn't have been the same without you.

Love,
Katie and Stan

In both of these examples, Katie and Stan's note is personal, but the second one is the truer expression of gratitude—and it's not that much longer. Don't be stingy with your sentiments.

Caring Deserves Caring

As you think about your thank-you notes, remember that everyone who gave a gift or helped you with your wedding plans did so because they care about you. Their thoughtfulness and good intentions are part of what you're acknowledging when you send them a note.

Take each note to heart, and consider both the gift and the giver. There is something unique about each gift, and something unique about the giver, even if it's a friend of your stepfather's whom you just met at the reception. Your stepfather was probably touched that he was there, and the fact that he came means he cares about you and your family. Be polite and sincere, follow the form of a thank-you note, and your job is done in spades. Here's an example of how to respond in such a situation:

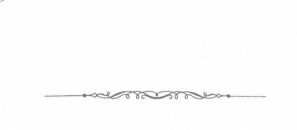

Dear Mr. Snyder,

Thank you very much for your generous gift of one hundred dollars. Roger and I have put it in a special savings account that will go toward buying our first house. We are excited about our future, and are so pleased you could join us for the wedding.

With our sincerest thanks,
Mary Ann Smith and Roger Leeds

A Note of Thanks

A fun thing about composing wedding thank-you notes is that as you go through the list, you will be writing not just formal notes, like the ones on the previous pages, but also notes that can even get silly or sappy, if they're for a friend with whom you have that kind of relationship. For example:

Dear Sandy and Nick,

What a delight to open your gift and find a pair of exquisite crystal candleholders. They will make even the simplest meal special for us at the end of a long day—and allow us to ignore any mess around the house that shall remain "unseen." They are just beautiful. Thanks, too, for sharing in our wedding. It was great to see you there.

Affectionately,
Ann and Barry

My Dearest Laura,

How did you know that I longed for the fuchsia champagne flutes that have been teasing me from the windows of Macy's for the entire summer? Oh, is it because I told you a hundred times how much I wanted them, that they would make the "perfect" wedding present for someone really special (such as myself)? You are so good at picking up on discreet signals!

Seriously, though, they are not only fabulously fun to look at and drink from, they will be forever a reminder of all that is wonderful about you. Their colorfulness, their sparkle, the way they bring happiness to the person who is drinking from them will make me think of you, my friend, every time.

For everything you've done for me and Cal through our engagement and wedding, I thank you from the bottom of my heart. And did you see the silver candlesticks at Crate and Barrel? How long until my birthday???

You're the best. Love ya,
Kris

OTHER SPECIAL WEDDING THANK-YOUS

You may have asked people to participate in your wedding in all sorts of ways, in the traditional role of bridesmaid or ring bearer, or the less traditional part of soloist or inspirational speaker, or even dog walker (to take care of your pooches during the ceremony). Anyone who did you a special favor should get a thank-you note.

Here's a sample note for the ring bearer:

Dear Hank,

Thank you for being our ring bearer at the wedding. You did such a good job, and you looked so handsome. It is a day we will remember forever, and it was made even more special because of you.

Thanks, buddy!
With all our love,
Sarah and Rob

For that special soloist, this is a note to inspire you how to thank her:

Dear Alice,

Wow did you sound great at our wedding! We were a little nervous about choosing "R-E-S-P-E-C-T" as our first "married" song, but not only did it help us relax and remember the early days when we would request that song at dances, but it got the rest of the wedding party in a celebratory mood, as well. We could tell that you put your heart and soul into it for us. Thank you!

We love you, girl!
Sarah and Rob

For your mom and dad, maybe you don't even need to see a note sample, but here is one anyway, heartfelt and sincere:

Dear Mom and Dad,

What can we say? Thank you doesn't quite cut it, but it's a start. You helped put together one of the most special days of our entire lives. From supporting our engagement and guiding us through the preparations to looking so great and being there with us through everything, we just can't tell you enough how much we love you and appreciate you.

Love,
Erin and Mark

To your unconditionally loving grandparents, here's some inspiration:

Dear Gran and Gramps,

Thank you for the set of cookware we registered for! It is a special gift for us, as we will use it often, and whenever we do we will think of you. Beyond the present, though, we want to thank you for all your love and support. You have always been there for us, and for that we are grateful beyond words. We look forward to sharing many more happy times together. We love you so much!

Time to use the pot you got us to make something good for dinner. Thinking of you always, with much love,

Jeannie and Luke

You may receive gifts for which you may not know how to express gratitude. It may be something you really don't like, is excessive, or something you have already received. Here are some tips for awkward instances:

Gifts You Don't Like
The items that fall into this category are plentiful—anything from linens in a color you despise to sushi dishes when you can't stand fish. The bottom line is that it doesn't really matter whether you like the gift or not, it's a gift and needs to be acknowledged as such. Avoid lying about liking the gift and focus instead on what it might be used for or a particular quality that it has. For example, saying something like "Thank you for the milk steamer. I know it will make a cup of coffee so much more enjoyable" isn't a lie. The giver doesn't need to know that you're not a coffee drinker and that it'll never be your cup of coffee.

Intangible Gifts

These include promises of using a beach house for a week or getting some shares of stock—things whose value may or may not pan out over time. They are still thoughtful gifts, however, and by acknowledging them, you also remind the giver that you are aware of the potential for the gift. For example, "Thank you for the offer of letting Andrew and me stay at your place in Cabo for a week. We are sure that with our busy schedules we will be needing a break, and it'll be a great retreat. We'll coordinate a time in the coming year. We so appreciate this generous gift!" A note like this can cement the deal while making the giver feel like it's truly appreciated.

Duplicate Gifts

Whatever the reason that you received the same gift from different people, don't let them know. Chalk it up to the occasion and send warm, individualized notes to both, or all, of the parties who sent you a set of ten turquoise napkins.

Gifts That Arrive Broken

Just as with a duplicate gift, the giver should be thanked without being told of the problem. If you know what store the gift came from, contact its customer service department about getting a replacement.

Group Gifts

When you receive something from multiple givers, they should each receive a personalized thank-you note. Don't send the same message to each person; think of something new to say to each one, even if it takes a while to think of something. The only exception to the group-rule is if it is particularly large—for example, if your whole office gets together and gives one gift, you can write one card to the office manager and ask him or her to share it with everyone.

A WORD TO THE WISE

Writing your first few thank-yous may be quite enjoyable, but as you work your way through your list you may find your enthusiasm waning. Procrastination may set in, as you somehow will always find something else to do. If you find yourself suddenly way behind schedule, make it priority number one to find the time to finish the job. Trust me, you do not want to suddenly run into Great Aunt Clare at a family function knowing that you never appropriately thanked her for her gift. Neither do you want to risk other potential fallout from this simple neglect, such as not being able to ask a friend of your parents' for a reference on a job, and so on. Laziness does have its consequences.

WEDDING NETIQUETTE

E-mail is a tricky area where wedding etiquette is concerned. Emilypost.com has definitive examples of when e-mail is acceptable and when it's not. Here are some wedding-related situations for which you shouldn't use e-mail:

* wedding invitations

* thank-you notes for gifts

* when discussing personal or thorny issues

In the following situations, e-mail is acceptable:

❋ "save the date" notices

❋ wedding RSVPs

❋ wedding announcements

❋ invitations to informal or casual engagement parties, bridal showers, or other get-togethers

❋ information on lodging

❋ wedding updates

Some words just sound so good together! If you're stuck, here are some tried-and-true phrases that will see you through your note.

To express gratitude for gifts think about the purpose, practicality, or pure pleasure of the gift when deciding what to say about it. Then follow through with phrases like:

✳ Just what I/we needed…

✳ A generous contribution…

✳ A welcome addition…

✳ The perfect accessory…

✳ A reminder of you…

✳ Just the right color…

✳ Makes my/our life easier…

✳ A great idea…

✳ Ideal in the living room/dining room/etc.…

✳ Complements my/our pattern/style/etc.…

✳ Comes at just the right time…

✳ Brightens up the room…

✳ Makes me/us happy…

✳ Something to treasure…

✳ A unique piece…

✳ The perfect choice…

✳ Totally me/us…

CHAPTER FIVE
Thank-You Notes for Other Occasions

"Thankfulness is the beginning of gratitude.
Gratitude is the completion of thankfulness.
Thankfulness may consist merely of words.
Gratitude is shown in acts."

—*Henri Frederic Amiel*

The best time to write a thank-you note is when
you are inspired by someone's generosity. Keep
in mind, though, that generosity doesn't always
come in the form of a package or present that
was given to you. Perhaps your child's bus
driver waited an extra few minutes when he or
she saw you doing your best to get to the stop on
time even though you were slightly late. Or
maybe your veterinarian suggested that you do
something for your pet that made a real difference in her health. Maybe a camp counselor was
a particularly positive influence in your child's
life over the summer. A thank-you note is a

wonderful way to let any of these people know they did something special for you or someone you love.

TYPES OF THANK-YOUS

Besides the impromptu occasions when a thank-you note seems like the right thing to do, there are times when they are a necessary courtesy. Those times include:

Gifts of Any Kind
You may feel that having your son or daughter say a big thank-you to Grandma for the jigsaw puzzle is enough, but Grandma would feel so much more special if she received a note in the mail from your child. A handwritten thank-you for this kind of casual gift may be considered a kind gesture, but for a more formal house-warming or anniversary present, a handwritten thank-you is obligatory.

Dinner Parties
When people extend themselves by having dinner parties, a note of thanks is always a good

idea, even if you contributed to the meal with a bottle of wine or a side dish.

Hospitality

Even close friends or family will appreciate a thank-you note for the hospitality they extended to you by welcoming your visit (no matter how short or long). It's the perfect time to compliment your hosts on something special about their home or their lifestyle that helped you appreciate or get to know them better.

Illness-Related and Condolence Gifts or Assistance

It may take some time before you feel up to it, but those who sent you gifts or donated their time to help you deserve your acknowledgment. If a death is involved, flowers, donations, even cards of condolence must be answered with thank-you notes.

Business

Sending a thank-you note after an interview may seem like an awkward, even dated, gesture, but it could also be the thing that secures you the job. Always follow up an interview with a thank-you note. The same is true for business gifts or entertainment.

Don't Be Late

How long do you have after receiving a gift or something for which you want to thank someone? It depends on the situation. Business interview thank-yous should be posted later that day or early the next so they arrive within a couple of days of the interview. Thank-yous for social niceties, general gifts, and other less formal occasions should be sent within a week of the occasion. Ideally, thank-you notes should be written as soon as possible so the sentiment is fresh and the gift-giver is suitably appreciated.

Here are the basic elements of a thank-you note:

Greeting
Use a salutation or a greeting to address the individual(s) to whom you are sending the note.

"Thank You"
Be sure to actually write "thank you" in the body of the note, even if the words already appear pre-printed on the note card you're sending.

Name of the Gift or Service
Identify the gift or reason for saying thank you. For example, a general "thank you for the lovely present" isn't quite right. It leads the gift-giver to believe that you either didn't really note the gift given, or that, maybe out of laziness, you were using a generic message on all your thank-you cards. Specifying the item or event is the way to properly express gratitude for it.

Feelings
Let the individual(s) know how you feel about the gift and what it might be used for or why you par-

ticularly like it. For example, you could say, "The First Christmas at Our New Home ornament is so special to us, not only because it is so pretty and so appropriate, but also because it is something we will come to treasure as we celebrate more and more Christmases here."

Personalization or Closing Sentence
The last sentence you write can sum up your feelings or be a more personal expression. Something like, "It was so nice to see you at Dad's surprise birthday party, and we will call you about getting together again soon."

Signature
Always include a closing salutation and sign your note. Within this framework, almost anything is possible, from the simplest of notes to the most heartfelt of greetings. Let your thoughts of the recipient of your note, as well as the occasion, guide you as you begin.

THE TONE OF YOUR NOTE

Keep these things in mind when determining the tone and purpose of the note:

* ❋ Why are you writing? What is the purpose of the note?

* ❋ Who is the recipient? A friend, family member (close or estranged), or couple?

* ❋ What is your relationship to the person or people?

* ❋ In thinking about the person or people, what personality traits come to mind? Does she have a playful side? Does he have a strong sense of humor? Let that sensitivity guide your writing, as well.

Keep in mind that formal or informal, you should be sincere, positive, and specific. Check your note for clarity and possible spelling mistakes before you seal the envelope. Be sure it says what you want and says it correctly.

Here is an example of a thank-you note that incorporates the basic elements and establishes a particular tone:

Dear Sue, [Greeting]

Thank you so much for the copies of the photos you made for me. ["Thank You"; Name the Gift] *The boys and I had so much fun with you and your kids that lovely summer day, and the photos are a wonderful way for us to always remember it. I am going to frame the three photos of the kids in the roller-coaster cars together as a montage and hang it on my photo wall, where we will see it all the time. What happy times!* [Feelings]

Thanks again for taking the time to come visit us, and we sure hope you'll come again soon. [Personalization]

Love,
Jen, Mark, and Ryan [Signature]

Salutations (Greetings)

For thank-you notes, the salutation or greeting you use is based on the formality of the occasion and your personal relationship to the recipient.

For close family or friends, using the first name or even a nickname is appropriate. Similarly, how you choose to address them can reflect the sentiment you wish to express as well as your relationship, and can vary from a sincere but fairly formal "Dear" to a conversational "Hey."

For formal situations and when addressing acquaintances, these conventions should be followed:

✳ Women may be addressed by Miss, Mrs., Ms., Madam, or by a professional title. Select what you feel the woman herself would prefer, and when in doubt, use Ms. Be aware of whether a married woman has taken her husband's last name, adopted a hyphenation, or kept her maiden name. Unmarried couples should be addressed by their individual names.

✳ Men should be addressed as Mr. unless they have a professional title. Use the full professional title and pay special attention to any abbreviations you may not be familiar with to be sure you use them correctly. This is especially important for business thank-yous; refer to the person's business card or see if there's an online company directory.

✳ When a couple includes two people with professional titles, be sure to include them both, as in "Dear Dr. and Senator Santos," "Dear Drs. Dyer," or "Dear Officer Michael Clark and Dr. Claire Clark."

A Note of Thanks

With an understanding of the basic form and function of the thank-you note, here is some advice to keep in mind while you're crafting notes for particular occasions.

Thank-Yous for Gifts

Gifts can be material objects or favors or services—such as when a neighbor picks up your kids after school and watches them while you are stuck in traffic, or when a friend brings you flowers because you're feeling down. In other words, gifts are anything that is given to you as an expression of courtesy or kindness. By sending a written note of thanks, you let the giver know that even a small gesture is one that made a difference for you...and they'll be most appreciative.

When writing a thank-you note for a gift, always consider your relationship to the giver. The secret is to put some of your personality on the paper; that is what people will be most happy to see in the notes they receive. In addition to following the basic format for any thank-you note, some simple rules to remember for these kinds of notes include:

✳ Mention the gift itself, what you will do with it, and how it makes you feel. Show appreciation for the article or act, even if the gift itself is not to your taste.

✳ Add a personal touch by writing down how you feel about the person who gave you the gift. Alternately, or in addition, let him, her, or them know what you've been doing lately, or something special that's happened to you or a loved one.

✳ Mention a past shared experience, a mutual friend, a favorite location— something that is truly personal.

✳ Be yourself. Don't use language that doesn't sound like you (if you wouldn't say "what a superb selection of chocolates," then don't write it), and don't be over-effusive if it's not sincere.

This may seem like a lot of rules for a simple thank-you note, but the fact is that not every note will need to be—or should be—long-winded. As long as each is from the heart, covers the bases, and is sent in a timely fashion, it will be well-received.

Here's an example of a to-the-point, three-sentence thank-you note:

Dear Luke,

Thank you so much for the electric foot warmer you sent for my birthday. Knowing how cold I sometimes get here at night, your gift was very thoughtful—especially coming from someone who lives in San Diego!

Hope all's well with you, and thanks again.

Fondly,
Ruth

Here's a five-sentence thank-you note:

Dear Audrey,

I can't wait to bundle up my baby in the beautiful blanket you gave me. I especially like the lambs that are embroidered on it! Because it has blue, pink, and yellow in it, it will go perfectly with any color scheme I select for the baby's room. (I'm a little behind on that!)

This is such an exciting time for me, and I give thanks every day that I have a friend like you to share it with. Twelve more weeks and I'll be a mom!

Lots of love,
Sharon

Here's an example of a formal thank-you note:

Dear Mr. and Mrs. Lander,

It was so kind of you to think of me upon my graduation from high school. I will need every penny when I head to college this fall, and I've put the twenty dollars you gave me into my "textbook fund" already.

Thank you very much for your generous gift.

Sincerely,
David

And here's an informal thank-you note:

Dear Alison,

You are such a nut! I can't believe you put together a surprise party for my birthday. How did you manage to get Larry to come—he is always busy! Of course he had to fly out to Vegas that night, but at least he was there. I haven't seen him since our reunion. Still looking good, isn't he?

Well, I loved everything about the party: from the fact that I didn't even know about it (amazingly enough), to the location (Sue and Tom's barn is such a great space), to the food (barbeque—my favorite!), to the band (you know how I love to dance).

Girl, I owe you big-time. You are such an awesome friend. You made turning forty fun, and now, instead of feeling old and wrinkly, I feel like I'm just getting started.

Thank you, thank you, from the bottom of my heart.

Love,
Tara

THANK YOUS FOR DINNER PARTIES

Don't you love those nights when you come home from a dinner party, which you weren't even particularly excited about going to, and feel like you shared some real quality time with old and new friends? An enjoyable dinner party is one of the great indulgences of life. If you come home feeling that way, don't hesitate to share your happiness with the host and hostess of the event. Dinner parties involve a lot of careful planning even if they're casual affairs, and your host and hostess will really appreciate that you enjoyed yourself. After all, that's why they had it!

Thank-yous for dinner parties follow the general rules for other thank-yous: Be specific about the event, share your feelings, cater your message to the relationship you have with the party givers, and include a nice closing. Because a dinner party is a fleeting, time-specific event, getting your card to the host and hostess as soon as possible is important. If you're a neighbor, hand deliver it the next day. Otherwise, be sure it's in the mail within a day or two, at most. Here are some examples for inspiration:

Dear Hal and Wendy,

We had such a wonderful time last night! Everything was special, from the drinks on the patio to the four-course meal in the dining room. The food just got better and better as the night went on, from the caviar-topped deviled eggs to the oysters to the pork roast—well, you know the menu, you created it. Inspired, for sure! The cheese course was a really fun idea, too. It made us feel like we were in Europe. Can we come to your house every Saturday night? Seriously, we know how much work goes into these things, and we wanted to extend an extra-special thank-you.

Appreciatively and fondly yours,
Rich and Janice

A Note of Thanks

Dear Sean, Diane, John, Ellie, and Sam,

What a special get-together that was last night! It is wonderful when these last-minute dinner plans work out. Of course the kids loved playing in the yard, and we are always delighted to catch up with you and reconnect. To me, a night like last night is what summer's all about. Thanks for being great hosts, great neighbors, and great friends.

Love,
Bill, Emily, Grace, and Cameron

Dear John and Elaine,

Carla and I wanted to thank you again for inviting us to your dinner party to meet David Reston. It is inspiring to meet someone who not only wants to make a difference in our community, but has the ideas and the support of local businesses to actually make them happen. We enjoyed everything about the evening, from the great food to the fine wines. It was generous and kind of you to host such an elegant and entertaining event. We hope to reciprocate sometime soon.

Sincerely,
Leonard and Carla Ross

A Note of Thanks

Whether your hosts set you up in a tent in the back-yard or in a private wing of their house, if they invite you or allow you to stay with them for any period of time, you should thank them in writing. If you visit your parents and bring the kids, this is a great time for you to write a note and have your kids do the same, then send the notes together. What a treat for your parents.

Regardless of whom you stayed with—or whether you brought a gift to them—a follow-up thank-you note is standard etiquette. Accommodating you (and perhaps even your family as well) involved extra planning and expense, and even though your hosts may have been very glad to do it, they went out of their way for you. A thank-you note is a simple and much-appreciated form of reciprocation.

When writing a hospitality thank-you note, remember that the "gift" is the hospitality. You should be specific about what it is you're thanking your hosts for. If you were on an extended stay, your note should necessarily be longer, as you will have more things to write about, but for a brief overnight visit, a couple of sentences is fine.

Here are some examples:

Dear Ann,

Thank you for letting me stay with you on my recent trip to New York. It was huge for me not to have to pay for a hotel. I spent the money on that suit, instead—sure hope it helped ace me the job interview!

It was a lot of fun catching up with you, too. I love what you're doing with your apartment—stay with the blue that you like for the kitchen, it's you! I really appreciated that you took the time to show me around your neighborhood. The Chinese food was fantastic.

I will let you know how the job search progresses, and I hope the next time I see you it will be because I, too, will be working in The Big Apple.

Fondly,
Lucy

A Note of Thanks

Dear Mom and Dad,

Thanks so much for making our annual summer visit to you another one that we will always treasure. We love going to the rocky beach so the kids can look for starfish and crabs, and you made sure we did just that— and had picnics to bring along! Now that the kids are old enough, it was really fun for them to go to the lighthouse. And thank you so much for providing paper, crayons, markers, Play-Doh, beads, and all the stuff that they love to play with. I am going to have the picture that Liza drew of your house framed so she can hang it in her room.

Dad, as always, your meals were feasts! Great barbeque, lots of fresh corn on the cob, and your desserts get better and better. Please send me the recipe for the simple chocolate cake you made—it was SO good!

The time went by so quickly. I can't believe we're home again, and school is starting in a week. We will keep you posted with news from Virginia, and look forward to seeing you at Thanksgiving.

Thanks again for everything.

With all our love always,
Brenda, Rich, Liza, Jason, and Hank

Dear Ed,

Thanks, man, for putting me up last night. It was nice to sleep on a bed after many nights crashing on couches. It was awesome waking up to coffee, too.
I'll call you when I get to L.A.

Talk to you later,
Jack

These examples should provide some help in writing a hospitality thank-you note. For more insight, Emily Post offers some advice on the matter in *Etiquette in Society, in Business, in Politics, and at Home*. She writes:

When you have been staying over Sunday, or for longer, in some one's house, it is absolutely necessary that you write a letter of thanks to your hostess within a few days after the visit.

"Bread and butter letters," as they are called, are the stumbling blocks of visitors.

Why they are so difficult for nearly everyone is hard to determine, unless it is that they are often written to persons with whom you are on formal terms, and the letter should be somewhat informal in tone. Very likely you have been visiting a friend, and must write to her mother, whom you scarcely know; perhaps you have been included in a large and rather formal house party and the hostess is an acquaintance rather than a friend; or perhaps you are a bride and have been on a first visit to relatives or old friends of your husband's, but strangers, until now, to you.

Don't be afraid that your note is too informal; older people are always pleased with any expressions from the young that seem friendly and spontaneous. Never think, because you can not easily write a letter, that it is better not to write at all. The most awkward note that can be imagined is better than none—for to write none is the depth of rudeness, whereas the awkward note merely fails to delight.

The sadness, stress, and grief of dealing with an extended illness or the loss of someone can often stifle the energy needed to write a thank-you note. However, anyone who was of particular service to you during an illness that you or someone you cared for suffered, or gifts or cards given as condolences should be acknowledged with a thank-you note.

Your note may be as simple as thanking a neighbor for picking up your kids and watching them for a couple of hours after school so you could go to the doctor's or get the extra sleep you needed to fight the flu. Maybe a friend sent an article that really made a difference to you when you were going through treatment for a major illness. Acts of kindness such as these can be acknowledged with casual but heartfelt thank-yous.

More formal notes need to be sent for condolences after someone's passing. When writing funeral-related thank-you notes, if someone's words of sympathy have truly touched you, let him or her know, and share something about the person whom you're both grieving.

Here's an example:

Dear Susan,

I was so touched to receive your note about my mom. Reading how much it meant to you that she would make us blueberry pancakes on Saturday mornings when you stayed over brought back those memories for me, too. Remember how much syrup we poured on those things? No wonder we could stay out in the snow all day—we were fortified!

I know my mom always liked it when you stayed over. I'm so glad we're still friends, and even though our lives have gone in different directions and we're not neighbors anymore, I think about you often.

Thanks again for your kind words and personal remembrances. They meant a lot to me.

Yours truly,
Alicia

Often, people send flowers, prepare food, or make monetary donations to a particular cause to remember a loved one. These gifts need to be acknowledged also. Here are a couple of examples to help you write notes for those occasions:

Dear Hannah and Len,

Thank you so much for the contribution you made to the American Cancer Society in Julia's name. The pain of losing her at such a young age is often more than we can bear, but knowing that research is being funded that may one day prevent others from experiencing this kind of loss is comforting. Bless you, and thank you for your kindness and support through everything.

Will all our love,
Carolyn and Michael

Dear Cindy,

Thank you for remembering Grace by sending the lovely bouquet of blue and yellow irises—her favorites—for the funeral. It was extremely thoughtful of you, and made a real difference in personalizing the difficult occasion.

This is a tough time for me. I miss Grace so much. It helps to have friends like you who understand.

With love,
Jeanne

There are numerous business-related situations that require a personal, handwritten thank-you note, and the people who honor this rule will find that it does pay off. These situations include job interviews, networking meetings, major purchases by customers, business-related social events, volunteer work, charitable contributions, mentoring assistance, and referrals. Essentially, any transaction or meeting that benefits you or your business should be acknowledged in as personal a way as possible.

Business thank-yous can often be more intimidating and complicated to write than other kinds of thank-yous, often because there is more on the line with a business note. How do you come across as grateful and enthusiastic with someone who has your future in his or her hands without seeming overbearing? How do you properly express your appreciation for someone's purchase without sounding like you're trying to make your next sale? When you send a note on company letterhead, you're representing not only yourself but your company, so you need to be sure also to reflect the interests of the organization. In order to avoid these pitfalls, it's important to craft your note with care and attention.

Below are some guidelines to follow when composing a business thank-you note.

Formalize It

This just means follow the standard rules for writing thank-you notes: say thank you, be specific, include a greeting and closing, and sign the note.

Personalize It

Even if you're representing your business to someone you don't personally know, the note is still coming from you and being sent to an individual. Do not send a form letter. Also, be yourself in the note. A friendly, conversational tone is what you're after.

Proofread It

Your college roommate may not mind finding a misspelling in a thank-you note that you write for a wedding gift, but you can be sure the executive who interviewed you for the job will. A business note demands correct spelling and grammar. If these are not your strong suits, be sure to have someone you trust proofread your note before you send it.

Write It Neatly

Just as the note should be error-free, it should also be easy to read. A customer won't be impressed with a note that can't be read because the handwriting is bad. This may mean slowing down or doing more than one draft.

Here's an example of a note sent to someone who donated time, prizes, or money:

Dear Dr. Fowler,

Thank you so much for your generous contribution to Stop Hunger Now! With gifts like yours, we will be able to feed many more during the upcoming holiday season. Thank you, as well, for volunteering to help serve meals in the Springer Shelter on Thanksgiving. I look forward to seeing you there.

Sincerely yours,
Lacey Randolph

Here's an example of a note sent in appreciation of a business lunch:

Dear Jane,

Thank you for taking the time to have lunch with me on Tuesday. It was very helpful for me to learn what you think are the real strengths and weaknesses of our industry, and how we should position our company with these factors in mind. I came back from lunch recharged to make some improvements with a new perspective on things.

I am keen on helping to take our company to the next level, and I truly appreciate your advice and assistance.

Sincerely,
Louisa

Next are two notes sent to customers who made major purchases:

Dear Ms. Jones,

I want to thank you for your recent purchase, and hope that the antique sideboard has found a wonderful new home with you where it will continue to be admired and treasured. It is a special piece.

I enjoyed talking about your experiences in the world of antiques—it is an addictive pastime! Again, thank you for visiting The Loft, and I hope to see you again.

Sincerely,
Anne Berrin

A Note of Thanks

Dear Mr. Evans,

I imagine you on the road in your new Volkswagen Passat, and I hope that you are enjoying it. Aren't the power and handling terrific? Wait until you get it up into the mountains and start driving some of those more twisty roads—it's exhilarating. Anyway, I hope that it is exceeding your expectations in all ways.

I wanted to say thank you again for choosing Hudson Volkswagen for your purchase. I hope your experience was a good one. If you have any questions or problems at any time, please feel free to contact me directly by phone, fax, or e-mail at the information listed on my business card. We pride ourselves on the service we provide after the sale, too, and our service department will be happy to answer any questions, as well.

When it comes time to consider another automobile, or if a friend is looking for a car, please consider Hudson.

Happy (and safe) driving!

Sincerely,
Jim Carver
Hudson Volkswagen

The essences of these notes is that they thank the people they're addressed to specifically for the purchase, gift, or service they provided; they are personalized; and they are to the point.

Closing Lines

There are numerous ways to sign off on a thank-you note, and, as the greeting, they depend on the formality of the situation and your relationship with the recipient.

* Respectfully,

* Sincerely,

* Respectfully yours,

* Sincerely yours,

* Most sincerely,

* Best wishes,

* With love,

* With much love,

* Kindest regards

* Your nephew,

* With blessings,

* With special thoughts for you,

* With my sincerest best wishes,

In mailboxes overstuffed with solicitations from all kinds of businesses, the handwritten note truly stands out. You can guarantee that a customer who receives a handwritten note will feel acknowledged and appreciated. Handwritten notes are also a must when acknowledging special kindnesses. For example, the boss who invited you to the company sales meeting or the owner of the shipping company who went out of his way to ensure your late shipment made it onto an earlier vessel. If you're the CEO or president of a company, you may want to send handwritten notes to your employees' homes, thanking them for specific examples of exceptional work.

Instances of when a typewritten thank-you note is appropriate include business-to-business communications and other occasions when additional formality is helpful or necessary. If your handwriting is truly terrible and you know it'll make a bad impression, typing your thank-you notes to your interviewers is a better option. Sending multiple notes of thanks for charitable donations can be somewhat redundant. Using a basic typewritten form letter and personalizing it for each donor is acceptable. (In these cases, it is critical to double-check that you have made all changes necessary between letters to be sure you don't forget to change a name or address.)

If you choose to type a thank-you note, you should use stationery-grade printer paper. Use standard 8½ x 11–inch paper and matching business-size envelopes. If you're writing the letter from your business, use business letterhead; if not, then type your address in the upper right-hand corner. Choose from among the following acceptable styles of formatting your letter:

✳ Blocked Style. Align the date and the clo-sing statement in the middle of the page. Indent each paragraph five spaces.

✳ Semi-Blocked Style. Align the date and the closing statement in the middle of the page. Beginnings of paragraphs are not indented.

✳ Full-Blocked Style. Everything is started at the left margin with no indentation. This includes the date, opening and closing statements, and text paragraphs. This is the style most commonly used today.

Regardless of the style, the body of the text should be single-spaced. There should be a line space after the salutation and before the closing statement. Two line spaces go between the closing statement and your typed name.

Here is an example of blocked style:

September 5, 2007

Dear Ms. Lane,

Thank you for choosing the Ghent Hilton as your guest hotel for your daughter's wedding. We are delighted to accommodate the party, and will do everything we can to make sure that the hotel experience is a wonderful part of the wedding. Please contact me with any questions or concerns you may have at any time before or during the scheduled stay. Best of luck with all the arrangements, and we'll see you next May!

Sincerely,
Barbara Reyes, Manager
Ghent Hilton

This is the same note in the semi-blocked style:

September 5, 2007

Dear Ms. Lane,

Thank you for choosing the Ghent Hilton as your guest hotel for your daughter's wedding. We are delighted to accommodate the party, and will do everything we can to make sure that the hotel experience is a wonderful part of the wedding. Please contact me with any questions or concerns you may have at any time before or during the scheduled stay. Best of luck with all the arrangements, and we'll see you next May!

Sincerely,
Barbara Reyes, Manager
Ghent Hilton

A Note of Thanks

Finally, here's what that note looks like in the full-blocked style:

September 5, 2007

Dear Ms. Lane,

Thank you for choosing the Ghent Hilton as your guest hotel for your daughter's wedding. We are delighted to accommodate the party, and will do everything we can to make sure that the hotel experience is a wonderful part of the wedding. Please contact me with any questions or concerns you may have at any time before or during the scheduled stay. Best of luck with all the arrangements, and we'll see you next May!

Sincerely,
Barbara Reyes, Manager
Ghent Hilton

With their potential significance, business letters carry should be especially carefully crafted. You might want to consider keeping several resource books on the subject handy.

E-MAIL NOTES

In a recent survey by the Emily Post Institute, 70 percent of the people polled responded "Yes" when asked if it was appropriate to send thank-you notes by e-mail. According to the Institute, "the comments submitted with both yes and no respondents indicated that viewers believe the decision about whether or not to send an e-mail thank you is situational. If the thanks is for a small gift, a favor, or some assistance given, e-mail is a reasonable choice."

Most contemporary etiquette advisories will say that an e-mailed thank-you is better than no thank-you at all. They also mirror the survey's findings saying that an e-mailed thank-you is appropriate "situationally." For example, if you're thanking someone you know fairly well for something minor—for example, you want to thank your child's teacher for spending some time after school with your child—an e-mail is acceptable. If you interview for a job with someone with whom your primary means of communication has been e-mail, then an e-mailed thank-you is appropriate.

Alison Doyle, the about.com careers columnist who has more than twenty years of experience in human resources, career development, and job searching, says that in most cases an e-mailed thank-you is acceptable. She explains, "You can get your thank-you letter out immediately, rather than have to wait for the postal service to deliver it. If the employer is making a quick hiring decision, time is of the essence. If there is no sense of urgency, you may still want to send a quick e-mail thank you, along with a traditional letter or note. You'll be reiterating your interest in the position sooner rather than later."

E-mailed thank-yous should follow all the rules of traditional thank-you notes. Be especially careful about spelling and punctuation with an e-mail, and double-check the e-mail address. It's easy to hit "send" before you've done a thorough proofing job.

While there is certainly precedence to support sending thank-yous by e-mail, don't forget the importance of sending handwritten notes.

Yes, some situational e-mails are acceptable, but remember that a thank-you note has a greater personal expression. E-mails are the kinds of notes you receive from people who are in a hurry, sending them in between other e-mail messages. The recipient of your e-mail is aware of this, if even just subliminally. There really is no substitute for the handwritten thank-you. After all, if you're going to gather your thoughts to thank someone, why not take the extra time and do it the old-fashioned and more proper way?

PRACTICE MAKES PERFECT

You'll find that there are many occasions that warrant a thank-you note. The areas covered in this chapter are a springboard for discovering and addressing those times. Like anything you want to learn or improve, practice is necessary. Don't be too hard on yourself with the first few thank-yous you write. You'll find that once you get the format down and feel comfortable with it, your feelings about the gift, the recipient, and the very act itself of writing, will take over and translate into a positive experience.

Helpful Hints

Suffering from writer's block? Here are some helpful words and phrases to get you started.

Words for Feelings

❋ delighted
❋ eager
❋ ecstatic
❋ excited
❋ flattered
❋ grateful
❋ happy
❋ humbled
❋ indebted
❋ overjoyed
❋ overwhelmed
❋ pleased
❋ thrilled
❋ touched

To Express Gratitude for Hospitality

* ❋ such fun!
* ❋ a memorable evening/weekend
* ❋ delightful company
* ❋ enjoyed myself/ourselves immensely
* ❋ thoroughly enjoyed
* ❋ a night to remember
* ❋ incredible cuisine
* ❋ outrageous meals
* ❋ made me/us feel so at home
* ❋ scintillating conversation
* ❋ welcome retreat
* ❋ taking such good care of me/us

To Express Gratitude for Condolences

* ❋ meant so much to me/us
* ❋ I/we appreciated your kind words
* ❋ being with me/us through this tough time
* ❋ sharing special memories with me/us
* ❋ supporting me/us
* ❋ helping with all the details
* ❋ your thoughts and prayers

To Express Gratitude for a Business-Related Gift

* your valuable time
* your excellent overview of the company
* your perspective
* your advice
* your generous gift
* your welcome contribution
* your thoughtful donation
* your continued support
* the wonderful things you have taught me
* helping me transition my career
* coaching me
* making this opportunity possible

CHAPTER SIX
Thank-You Notes from Children

"Gratitude is not only the greatest of virtues, but the parent of all the others."

—*Marcus Tuillius Cicero*

If receiving a thank-you note from an adult is special, receiving one from a child has to be one of life's greatest simple pleasures. A friend, relative, teacher, or coach all will appreciate receiving notes of thanks from your children. And the fact is, your child will be held in higher regard by these people, who are influential in his or her life, when your child expresses thanks for a gift.

Beyond the positive feelings that your child's thank-you notes will give their recipients is the important life lesson your child is learning by writing the notes, which is that expressing gratitude is a very valuable and rewarding habit.

FORMING THE HABIT

As nice as all this sounds—and as true as it is—developing the habit of writing thank-you notes in your child or children is not easy. Especially today, when it's uncommon to receive written thank-you notes. Since children are e-mailing friends and family at younger ages, you can expect your child to come into the task reluctantly at best, and sometimes quite defiantly.

There may be times when you will simply have to force your child to complete the thank-you note or notes, but there are ways to make the task more enjoyable for everyone, including yourself.

THE THANK-YOU NOTE BOX

If you've followed the advice in this book, you have created a box of special thank-you note stationery, pens, and perhaps some items to decorate your cards with. Kids will love putting something like this of their own together. Get an old shoebox and cover it with paper of some kind—anything from a favorite giftwrapping to brown, plain, or colored construction paper that the child can decorate him- or herself.

Go to a stationery store together or shop online to find both preprinted boxed cards and age- and gender-appropriate stationery. You can even craft your own cards together by making them out of the child's favorite colors of construction paper, or creating something on the computer that can be printed out. The possibilities are many, though the paper should reflect the "weight" of the occasion—friends, family members, teachers, and people you know well may appreciate homemade cards, but others, such as distant relatives or your business associates, may require a more traditional approach.

Include some favorite stickers or invest in a set of stamps and special-colored inks that your child can use to put on the envelopes. Depending on your child's age, you can decide whether a special pen or set of markers is necessary, or whether the household ballpoints will suffice. (Cartridge pens, fat-tipped markers, even fine-tipped crayons are all intriguing choices, but will typically be either too difficult to manage properly or will detract from the impact of the message. A simple ballpoint pen is best for the letter itself; reserve decoration for the card and/or envelope.)

When your child's stationery box is completed, give him or her a self-stick label on which to write his or her name and use to personalize the box. Think of someone to write a note to right away, while the excitement of the box is still strong for your child. Select a special card or paper, give your child a pen, and let the writing begin! The specialness of the box and the new things in it should give note writing a positive association. Be available for your child as he or she crafts the note, in case there are any spelling questions or you need to offer specific reminders about the gift or occasion. Congratulate your child's efforts. When the task is complete, put your child's box in a place where there won't be the temptation to get it out and play with it along with other craft supplies.

MAKING IT HAPPEN

Children can begin writing thank-you notes as soon as they can read and write—starting in kindergarten or first grade. Young children will necessarily need more help while they're creating their notes; older children will probably need more help to simply follow through and get the job done.

Baby Notes

Don't let the fact that you have an infant or a toddler keep you from letting gift-givers know that their presents were appreciated. Whenever someone gives something to your baby, a thank-you note is in order. If your child is too young to write, you will need to write the note for him or her. If your child is old enough, you can have him or her scribble something at the bottom to personalize the note. If not, then sign the card with his or her name. Of course, the gift-giver will know it's from you, but will enjoy thinking it's from your little angel. (The exception to this is if the present is indeed for you, even if it's something baby related. In this case, the note should come from you.)

A proper thank-you note can't be written between breakfast bites, while waiting for the bus, watching TV, or playing video games. Like doing homework, writing a thank-you note requires a (relatively) quiet, clear, and distraction-free space. You can't expect your child to do a good job if you haven't given him or her a suitable time and space in which to do it. On the other hand, writing a thank-you note shouldn't become something so "special" that the expectations going into it end up being too intimidating.

As the parent, you should choose what you consider an appropriate time. It shouldn't be when your child is too hungry, sleepy, or anxious to go outside and play. Depending on how many notes you have to write, you'll have to think of how much time you'll need. A single note can take ten to thirty minutes, and sometimes even longer, depending on how detailed or decorated the note gets. Sending notes to everyone who gave a birthday present may take several hours. Large tasks should be broken up to be done properly.

So that your child has both some personal space and access to you during the writing process, the best place to work is probably at the kitchen table. Clear a large enough area and don't eat or drink until the job is done. Get out the special box, give your child a pen, and let him or her go at it!

COVERING THE BASICS

A child's thank-you note should follow the same guiding principles of all thank-you notes and should include:

⁕ proper opening and closing phrases
⁕ the words "thank you"
⁕ specifics about the gift
⁕ something personal
⁕ a signature

The following examples of notes are of different lengths and cover a range of occasions. The grammar and spelling are correct because they are published in this book, but keep in mind that it's rare to see children's thank-you notes without misspellings or some incorrect grammar. That's okay. Be sure people's names are spelled correctly and the gift is correctly identified. Otherwise, let the little stuff go.

The most common reason your child will need to write a thank-you note will be to express gratitude for birthday or holiday gifts—or gifts given for no reason at all. Make sure you keep a list of who gave each present so that there's no uncertainty when it comes to actually writing the notes. You don't want to thank someone for a gift they didn't give! Here are some examples of children's thank-you notes for a gift—again, brief is good as long as you cover all of the basic points.

Dear Aunt Lu,

Thank you for the Power Ranger pajamas for my birthday. They are the best! Say hi to Maggie for me.

Love,
Andrew

Dear Joey,

Thank you for coming to my birthday party. You are my best friend. I can't wait to use the gift certificate for the toy store. I am going to buy the Star Wars video game. We can play it.

Your friend,
Sam

If your child had a positive experience on a sports team, a note to the coach will be much appreciated. This kind of note can be fun to write if you use a sports-related stationery, like a note pad with a soccer ball on it, or you create a card together on the computer, finding favorite sports-related images. You can even paste magazine pictures around the edges or include a team photo. Get creative! Here are some examples:

Dear Coach Lisa,

Thank you for being such a good coach for soccer. I had so much fun this season. I learned a lot, especially about ball control. I miss you and the team and can't wait for next season. Go Flames!

Sincerely,
Robin

Dear Coach Sammy,

I really liked baseball this year. It was fun. You are a nice coach. I hope you are my coach next year.

Your friend,
Michael

Then there's the overnight visit, which certainly deserves a follow-up thank-you note. Writing this kind of note helps complete the experience on a very positive note, and might even convince the caretakers to do it again.

Dear Grandma and Grandpop,

Thank you for taking care of me while my mom and dad were away. I love staying at your house. You make the best pancakes.

I especially liked when we went to see the army boat. That was cool.

I love you,
Robert

Dear Uncle Fred,

I had such a good time at your house. I like playing Xbox with you and Nick. Thank you for letting me stay at your house this weekend. Can I come stay with you again soon?

Love,
John

Sometimes your children will encounter other individuals—doctors, babysitters, camp counselors, bus drivers, or flight attendants—who made a positive difference for them by doing something small or routine. How wonderful for these folks to receive a note of thanks from your child! Letting someone know they made a difference by thanking them in writing is inspirational for everyone. Here are several such thank-yous to provide inspiration:

A Note of Thanks

Dear Dr. Raines,

Thank you for being so nice to me when I broke my arm. I was scared, and you made me feel okay. You were right. It doesn't hurt that much. I liked being able to pick out the color of my cast. You are a great doctor.

Thank you,
Lara

Dear Mrs. Stewart,

Thank you for being such a nice teacher. It was fun to be in your class. I am a little scared of going into the third grade and seeing who my new teacher will be. Can I come visit you?

Thank you for the book about the dinosaurs. I like T Rex the best. Do you?

Your student,
Matthew Stanton

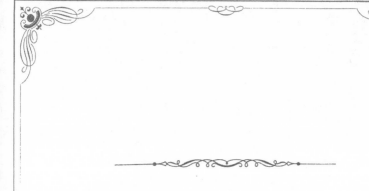

Dear Courtney,

I have so much fun when you babysit. You are the best!
Thank you for bringing over your favorite movies to share with
me and for teaching me the card trick.

Your friend,
Nicholas

A Note of Thanks

Here's an example of a note that you might be lucky enough to receive from your child one day or that may make you consider writing a note of thanks to your own mom or dad to express gratitude for everything they've done for you over the years.

Dear Mom,

Thank you for everything that you do for me every day. You have a lot to take care of, but you always have time for me. I was so glad you could sew the patches on my jacket before school this year, and even though I sometimes get embarrassed, I like finding your notes in my lunch box. I really like playing cards and watching movies together.

You are the best. I love you so much.

Happy Mother's Day!
Your daughter,
Rachel

Your child may experience many emotions while writing the note. First, he or she may be writing it because it is something that you said had to be done. Therefore, the task might be viewed as a chore not to be enjoyed. Second, your child has to think of something to say, and of how to spell the words. Thinking about the person and/or gift may be a happy or confusing experience, and may even lead to a greater "life" discussion between the two of you.

For example, if your son didn't especially like staying with your parents while you were away, he still needs to send them a thank-you note. This is a time to talk about the importance of being polite and having good manners. It's also an appropriate time for you to find out more about what may have upset your child. If it's something serious, it's important that you know about it.

Just remember that what you've asked your child to do falls outside of what's normal for kids today. Your attitude through the whole thing will influence your child tremendously both as the note is being written and in how he or she approaches the task in the days, months, and years to come. Keep these things in mind:

✳ Don't be overly critical. Grandma will be thrilled with almost any effort.

✳ Don't be too permissive, either. A scribbled, generic "thank you" isn't enough and will reinforce a bad habit—and won't instill the real meaning behind writing a thank-you note.

✳ Don't get into a power struggle. If the note-writing degenerates into you threatening your child, simply put the materials away and let him or her know the job will need to be done at another time. Give your child or yourself a time-out and start over when both of you are in a better mood.

✳ Set up a reward system for a job well done. Letting your child have an extra half-hour of TV time or a special dessert may be the reward for tackling multiple thank-yous; and certainly, a big hug and a kiss should follow the writing of even a simple note. Kids are very reward-driven, and any positive effort should be acknowledged and rewarded. The point is for you to express your approval, and the way to do that is with a big hug or a favorite snack for your child.

✳ Consider writing together. If you don't have a thank-you to write, take the time to write a postcard or a letter to someone. Let your child see what you've written, perhaps even let him or her include something in your letter. Be an example for your child that writing to someone is easy and special.

✳ Let your child pick out her own stamps. There are all kinds of stamps that are appealing to kids, from designs like flowers or crafts to super heroes or baseball players. Let your child put the stamp on the envelope and even address it, if you trust that the handwriting will be legible. When you go to the post office, let your child put the note in the mailbox or slot. Though we see these things as mere conveniences, to our kids they are "grown up" things that are special.

✳ In the wonderful words of Carl Jung, remember that, "An understanding heart is everything in a teacher, and cannot be esteemed highly enough. One looks back with appreciation to the brilliant teachers, but with gratitude to those who touched our human feeling. The curriculum is so much necessary raw material, but warmth is the vital element for the growing plant and for the soul of the child." Think of this when you're helping your child, whether it's with the task of doing homework, participating in sports, or writing thank-you notes.

When your children are young, you will likely be the one to get the most satisfaction out of this process. As it becomes more routine and your children see how happy their efforts make the people to whom they write their thank-yous, the process will become self-fulfilling for them, too. Your support and encouragement will pay off!

CHAPTER SEVEN
*Thank-You Notes and Writing Longer Letters
and Other Correspondence*

**"Gratitude unlocks the fullness of life. It
turns what we have into enough, and more. It
turns denial into acceptance, chaos to order,
confusion to clarity. It can turn a meal into a
feast, a house into a home, a stranger into a
friend. Gratitude makes sense of our past,
brings peace for today, and creates a vision
for tomorrow."** —*Melody Beattie*

It just may happen that writing thank-you notes
inspires you to write down more of your
thoughts and feelings. If that's the case, how
wonderful for your friends and family! Just as
penning thank-yous can put you in touch with
how you feel about people who give you gifts or
provide services for you, so taking the time to
write a letter to someone can bring you insights
into all sorts of things.

With a box of personalized stationery or note cards, a favorite pen, and a special friend in mind, you are ready to undertake a journey of connection and appreciation. Think of your friend as though he's in the room with you, tell him about something special that happened to you, or something you're concerned about, or you can even recount the day's events. You may be surprised by the thoughts that come to you. In the end, if you feel you've written something inappropriate—say you realized that you have described someone in very negative terms—you can always put the letter aside and not send it. You will still have had the opportunity and experience of tapping into certain feelings. Emily Dickinson said it nicely: "It is cold tonight, but the thought of you is so warm, that I sit by it as a fireside, and am never cold any more. I love to write to you—it gives my heart a holiday and sets the bells to ringing."

That's what's wonderful about writing and receiving letters—they warm the heart and excite the senses. My sons learned how to formally compose a letter in second grade, and part of their homework was to send a letter to someone in their class. While they wrote their notes somewhat grudgingly (it was homework, after all), they were thrilled when they received letters from their classmates.

We went away one summer, and one of my sons especially missed one of his friends from school. I encouraged him to write to him, which he did. He even addressed the envelope, put the stamp on it, and gave it to the man at the post office. He did this not knowing if he was going to get a reply, but a few weeks later, when an envelope addressed to him appeared in our mailbox, the joy and excitement he experienced just holding the letter made the whole process worthwhile. He treasured that letter, and it inspired him to write others.

What can a letter do that a telephone call or e-mail can't? First, writing a letter necessitates that time is taken to reflect upon and compose thoughts without interruption or distraction. Yes, it's nice to be able to hear someone's voice, and be able to discuss something in the present, but writing a letter is a more intimate act. It allows you to share a special part of yourself with someone. An e-mail, while it can be detailed, doesn't have the intimate feel of a letter. The essential nature of an e-mail is its functionality—to deliver a message quickly. It's a convenience, not a gift.

Unlike thank-you notes—which follow a certain form and need to be correct in every way, especially in business situations—a letter can take almost any form. Growing up, my friends and I used to write to each other in different shapes, using sentences to create circles, ovals, animals, and so on. The paper had to be turned as the sentences were written and read, making the letters that much more special. It may be consoling for you to learn that Abraham Lincoln was a terrible speller, or that Katherine Mansfield's handwriting was practically illegible. Don't worry about crossed-out words or changing pens midstream. Make drawings in the margins or use smiley faces if you want.

You can even write a letter as a warm-up to writing a thank-you note. The spontaneity of it can help you loosen up, just as an athlete might stretch before a competition. There are always reasons to let someone know you're thinking of them by writing to them. Here are just a few ideas:

✳ Drop your mom and dad a quick note to let them know how much you care about them—even if you speak with one or both of them often.

✳ Surprise your spouse with a note tucked into a coat pocket or a pocketbook, or send him or her a card at the office. Try your hand at a love letter—a whole new way of declaring your love may await you!

✳ When you come across a photo or article in a magazine or newspaper that reminds you of someone, cut it out and send it to them with a short (or long) letter.

✳ Leave letters on your teenager's door. It's so hard to talk to adolescents sometimes. Even if they tell you they don't appreciate your notes, they do, and it is something they'll look back on with fondness—even twenty years later!

✳ Put notes in your child's lunchbox for school. Elementary school kids love notes of encouragement, middle school kids love mysteries or riddles, and older kids appreciate reminders of social engagements or things they can look forward to.

✳ Send a letter to a friend you've been out of touch with—or one you spend a lot of time with. Take your relationship to a new level.

✳ Keep a stack of postcards handy and try to send one regularly (once a week or once a month) to someone special.

✳ Send a letter from your whole family to another family you're friends with but don't get to see very frequently. Include photos or drawings to make it even more special.

READING OTHER PEOPLES' LETTERS

When letter writing was the primary way for people to express themselves to others, letters were more highly scrutinized in certain circles. They were judged on the type of stationery used, as that was a first impression. But once that initial evaluation was made, it came down to seeing how a letter was written. Grammar, style, and tone all contributed to whether a letter was considered well-written or not. Emily Post weighed in heavily on how to not only pen proper English, but where to find good examples of it. As she wrote in 1922:

> There is no better way to cultivate taste in words than by constantly reading the best English. None of the words and expressions which are taboo in good society will be found in books of proved literary standing. But it must not be forgotten that there can be a vast difference between literary standing and popularity, and that many of the "best sellers" have no literary merit whatsoever.

NEVER SAY	CORRECT FORM
1. In our residence we retire early (or arise)	1. At our house we go to bed early (or get up)
2. I desire to purchase	2. I should like to buy
3. Pardon me!	3. I beg your pardon. Or, Excuse me! Or, sorry!
4. Lovely food	4. Good food
5. Elegant home	5. Beautiful house—or place
6. A stylish dresser	6. She dresses well or she wears lovely clothes
7. Charmed! or Pleased to meet you!	7. How do you do!

NEVER SAY	*CORRECT FORM*
8. Attended	8. Went to
9. I trust I am not trespassing	9. I hope I am not in the way (*unless trespassing on private property is actually meant*)
10. Request (*meaning ask*)	10. Used only in the third person in formal written invitations
11. Will you accord me permission?	11. Will you let me? *or* May I?
12. Permit me to assist you	12. Let me help you
13. Brainy	13. Brilliant *or* clever
14. I presume	14. I suppose
15. Tendered him a banquet	15. Gave him a dinner
16. Converse	16. Talk
17. Partook of liquid refreshment	17. Had something to drink
18. Perform ablutions	18. Wash
19. A song entitled	19. Called (*proper if used in legal sense*)
20. I will ascertain	20. I will find out
21. Residence *or* mansion	21. House, *or* big house
22. In the home	22. In some one's house *or* At home
23. Phone, photo, auto	23. Telephone, photograph, automobile

A Note of Thanks

To be able to separate best English from merely good English needs a long process of special education, but to recognize bad English one need merely skim through a page of a book, and if a single expression in the left-hand column following can be found (unless purposely quoted in illustration of vulgarity) it is quite certain that the author neither writes best English nor belongs to Best Society.

Besides offering lists of comparative phrases that could be considered appropriate or proper, Ms. Post also directed letter writers to seek greater purity in their speech by further refining their vocabulary. She writes:

"Tintinnabulary summons," meaning bell, and "Bovine continuation," meaning cow's tail, are more amusing than offensive, but they illustrate the theory of bad style that is pretentious…. Many other expressions are provincial and one who seeks purity of speech should, if possible, avoid them, but as "offenses" they are minor:

Reckon, guess, calculate,
    or figure, meaning think.
Allow, meaning agree.
Folks, meaning family.
Cute, meaning pretty or winsome.
Well, I declare! Pon my word!
Box party, meaning sitting in a
    box at the theater.
Visiting with, meaning talking to.

There are certain words which have been singled out and misused by the undiscriminating until their value is destroyed. Long ago "elegant" was turned from a word denoting the essence of refinement and beauty into gaudy trumpery. "Refined" is on the verge. But the pariah of the language is culture! A word rarely used by those who truly possess it, but so constantly misused by those who understand nothing of its meaning, that it is becoming a synonym for vulgarity and imitation. To speak of the proper use of a finger bowl or the ability to introduce two people without a blunder as being "evidence of culture of the highest degree" is precisely as though evidence of highest education were claimed for who ever can do sums in addition, and read words of one syllable. Culture in its true meaning is widest possible education, plus especial refinement and taste.

The fact that slang is apt and forceful makes its use irresistibly tempting. Coarse or profane slang is beside the mark, but "flivver," "taxi," the "movies," "deadly" (meaning dull), "feeling fit," "feeling blue," "grafter," a "fake," "grouch," "hunch" and "right o!" are typical of words that it would make our spoken language stilted to exclude.

All colloquial expressions are little foxes that spoil the grapes of perfect diction, but they are very little foxes; it is the false elegance of stupid pretentiousness that is an annihilating blight which destroys root and vine.

In the choice of words, we can hardly find a better guide than the lines of Alexander Pope:

> In words, as fashions, the same
>   rule will hold;
> Alike fantastic, if too new, or old:
> Be not the first by whom the
>   new are tried,
> Nor yet the last to lay the old aside.

Perfect simplicity and freedom from self-consciousness are possible only to those who have acquired at least some degree of cultivation. For simplicity of expression, such as is unattainable to the rest of us, but which we can at least strive to emulate, read first the Bible; then at random one might suggest such authors as Robert Louis Stevenson, Agnes Repplier, John Galsworthy and Max Beerbohm. E. V. Lucas has written two novels in letter form—which illustrate the best type of present day letter writing.

A Note of Thanks

I think we can all be relieved that times change! Of course you want to write well, spell correctly, and express yourself in ways that make you look good, not silly. But whichever form of letter writing you choose, trust that your efforts will not go unappreciated by the receiver and, perhaps surprisingly, by your own self. A heartfelt, sincere letter to anyone is an act of kindness and good faith in the world.

"I would maintain that thanks are the highest form of thought, and that gratitude is happiness doubled by wonder."

—*G. K. Chesterton*

RESOURCES

Below is a short list of titles on the topics of letter writing and etiquette. Several of these books were used as reference material, while others are simply recommended reading. Hundreds of books on both topics can be found in libraries, bookstores, and through Internet retailers.

Aresty, Esther B. *The Best Behavior: The Course of Good Manners from Antiquity to the Present—As Seen Through Courtesy and Etiquette Books.* NY: Simon & Schuster, 1970.

Devlin, Joseph, MA. *How to Speak and Write Correctly.* NY: The Christian Herald, 1910.

Editors of Victoria Magazine. *Writing Personal Notes and Letters.* NY: Sterling Publishing Co., Inc., 1998.

Goodwin, Gabrielle, and David Macfarlane. *Writing Thank-You Notes: Finding the Perfect Words.* NY: Sterling Publishing Co., Inc., 1999.

Lamb, Sandra E. *Personal Notes: How to Write from the Heart for Any Occasion.* NY: St. Martin's Press, 2003.

Leas, Connie. *The Art of Thank You: Crafting Notes of Gratitude.* NY: Beyond Words Publishing, 2002.

Martin, Judith. *Miss Manners' Guide to Excruciatingly Correct Behavior.* NY: Warner Books, 1982.

— — —. *Miss Manners' Guide for the Turn-of-the-Millennium.* NY: Pharos Books, 1989.

Post, Elizabeth L. *Emily Post on Etiquette.* NY: Harper & Row, 1987.

Post, Emily. *Etiquette in Society, in Business, in Politics, and at Home.* NY: Funk & Wagnalls, 1922.

ACKNOWLEDGMENTS

A book about thank-you notes wouldn't be complete without its own thank-yous! First, to Pamela Horn at Sterling for giving me the opportunity to write this book, and to my editor, Joelle Herr, for her own wise words while the book was in progress.

A special thanks to my family—Carlo, Dawson, Dylan, Chief, Chelsea, and Cinderella. I could never run out of reasons to say thank-you to every one of you, every single day. You know I mean it!

The one I need to thank the most is my mother, Evelyne Hoover, whose own love of writing letters of all kinds inspired me from an early age. I may be one of the few people who can interpret her handwriting, but that's because I've read so many of her letters. All of them make my heart sing and my spirit soar. I hope there will be many more. *Merçi, maman.*

INDEX

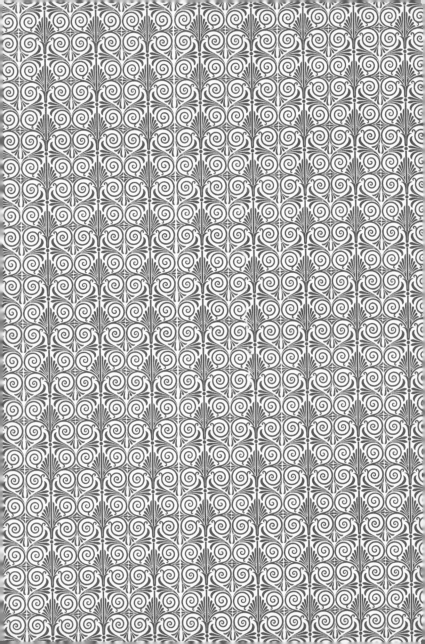